COMMON MISTAKES IN CHRISTENDOM

NGRIME DIVINE NJELOWE

Leavitt Peak Press

ISBN: 978-1-957956-26-8 (sc)
ISBN: 978-1-957956-27-5 (e)

Rev. date: 08/03/2022

Contents

Dedication

To the HOLY GHOST, my Teacher

To the Fiango Assembly of Liberty Ministry International

To all lovers of Gospel truth

To my dear wife, OLENGE BERTHA

And my daughters, BLESSINGS, ZOE, HARMONY and CELESTIAL.

Foreword

IN THE BODY OF CHRIST, whatever does not pass the test of the word of God is not fit to stay relevant; no matter the level or degree of acclamation it receives. When it comes to God, human wisdom doesn't count: what counts is His word. Thus, we must align whatever we have to do before Him to His written word.

We must understand that most often, what is good for us may not be good for God. We must as well understand that making our man-made doctrines more popular than the prescription of God's word does not negate Bible truth in any way. Truth remains truth, and cannot remain buried forever.

But what happens to those who muscle the courage to point to the right direction while all others point towards the opposite end? They are black mailed, nicknamed, hated, and treated with scorn. Yet, like in the case of king Ahab and Prophet Micaiah in the Bible (2 chronicles 18:1-34), the truth will always triumph.

Knowledge is good; very good. But the processing of knowledge is as well of utmost importance. In the process of knowledge acquisition, do you accept all that is given to you as Bible truth?

"That very night the believers sent Paul and Silas to Berea. When they arrived there, they went to the Jewish synagogue. And the people of Berea were more open-minded than those in Thessalonica, they listened eagerly to Paul's message. They searched the scriptures day after day to see if Paul and Silas were teaching the truth." Acts 17:10-11 (NLT).

The Berean method of receiving the word and proving it true or false is the best in the world we live in today, which has so many teachers and preachers of the word like me.

I have simply given you the formula; you are not bound to accept all what is written on the pages of this book. You have the exclusive right to cross-examine, evaluate, judge, and assimilate or reject what you read here. This book is not the Bible itself, it's just a piece of work based on Biblical teachings.

However, I urge you to buy the truth, and sell it not. We have to be honest to ourselves at times and accept truth, no matter how it hurts. Usually, the medicine that hurts in the wound is what treats it faster.

Finally, if the message contained in this book blesses you, then share it: don't keep it to yourself, and God will bless you. Thanks.

Pastor Ngrime Divine Njelowe

Acknowledgement

I AM DEEPLY GRATEFUL TO all those who have been my teachers either directly or indirectly, at one time or the other.

I owe much thanks to the Apostolic Church Cameroon (T.A.C.C) and the Ndian District in particular, who acted like a mid-wife during my spiritual birth process, and a nursing mother to me as a young convert.

Immeasurable thanks and gratitude to Prophet Sem Eric, my mentor and spiritual father, and the Liberty Ministry International Family. Thank you for giving me a platform. Am indebted to you.

No man can succeed alone. No matter how anointed or gifted you are, you need the help of others to achieve success. Mr/Mrs Ngwa Divine Suh, am talking of people like you. This work could not have been possible without your support.

I will not fail to make mention of some of my fathers in the faith like Pastor Ngah Edward, Pastor Peter Atabong, Pastor Ediage Valerie and late Pastor Su-uh Christopher. They were, and have been a source of inspiration to me.

My sincere thanks to faithful brethren in Christ, who stood by me to foster this gift, in the persons of Elder Lebaga Stanislaus Kila,

Mummy Atabong Maurine, Pastor Njibili Collins, Doctor Ronald Gobina, Sister Frida Wose, Elder Imbimbe Richard, Elder Henry Nyaba, Brother Paul Meboka and a host of others.

I will not forget the unflinching support of my wife, her family and mine. May God bless you all. Thank you Sister Bernice, for typing my work. Thanks to you, Sister Marvelous Joy, for praying and believing in me.

Introduction

THE SARCASTIC USE OF THE word "Christendom" in the title of this work, is enough to tell us that mistakes are only possible, and can get to the uncommon level of being common in Christianity, and not in the body of Christ.

The body of Christ (the church) is a perfect body: pure, holy, incorruptible, sanctified and without spots or wrinkles

> *"And you husbands, show the same kind of love to your wives as Christ showed to the church when He died for her, to make her holy and clean, washed by baptism and God's word; so that he could give her to himself as a glorious church without a single spot or wrinkle or any other blemish, being holy and without a single fault."* Ephesians 5:25-27 (TLB).

As seen in the scripture above, the reason why Christ died on the cross is to make the church (His Body) holy, cleansed by water and the word, that she might be without spot or wrinkle, or any other defect.

This therefore emphasizes the need of constant preaching and teaching of the word, which is the main ingredient that cleanses the church from all filths and imperfection; thereby giving credence to works like this in your hand.

The word of God remains the word of God, even if it's coming from the mouth of a babe, or an insane person. Its infallibility and spiritual potency remains the same. And like looking at the mirror, we should be able to see ourselves through the word, and be able to make adjustments that are needed in our love walk with Him.

However, our major challenge as children of the kingdom is not the devil (who is a defeated foe), but our inability to yield our spirits to the written and spoken word of God, that is able to build us up to a perfect man in Christ.

> *But now is the time. Never forget the warning, 'today if you hear God's voice speaking to you, do not harden your hearts against Him, as the people of Israel did when they rebelled against Him in the desert.'* " Hebrews 3:15 (TLB).

The choice for change has always been ours to make. Nevertheless, whether we make that decision or not, change will definitely have its way in the affairs of men.

As you peruse through the pages of this book, my desire is for you to learn, and be able to come to the knowledge of the truth. Shalom.

Chapter One

YOU'RE NOT A CHRISTIAN

THE SIMPLE QUESTION, "WHO ARE you?" has had one of the most perplexing answers in the entire history of the human race. And believe it or not, the majority of people today on earth do not know who they really are. Obviously, each time you start pondering anew of who you truly are, will definitely lead you to a new discovery of yourself.

It is as well obvious that most of those around you (almost 90% of them) don't know who you truly are. Humans are the most complex of all of God's creation. You can hardly tell who a man truly is, or what he thinks.

Who and what defines you matters a lot. It took only God Himself to reveal to us who Jesus really is. Even the disciples who had been with Him, and had maintain very close contact with Him couldn't give definite answers to the question about His personality.

> *"When Jesus came to the region of Caesarea Philipi, He asked His disciples, "who do people say the Son of Man is?" They replied, "some say John the Baptist; others say Elijah; and still others, Jeremiah or one of the prophets." "but what about you?" He asked. "who do you say I am?" Simon peter answered, "You are the Christ, the Son of the living God." Jesus replied, "Blessed are you, Simon son of Jonah, for this was not revealed to you by man, but by my Father in heaven."* Matthew 16:13-17 (NIV)

Jesus was amazed at Peter's answer, but knew exactly where the answer came from: God had revealed it to him. Therefore, it is enough to say that even as believers, we must go to God for us to truly know who we are.

It is very wrong to identify children of God by the name "Christian"; and since God opened my understanding of it, it irritates me to hear the word mentioned. But where did the name come from? Who gave us the name and why? What is the meaning of the name Christian, and how does it fall short of scriptural truths? If we are not Christians then who are we? We will address all of these concerns here one after the other. The word "Christian" was first used in Acts 11:26,

> *"And when he had found him, he brought him to Antioch. So it was that for a whole year they assembled with the church and taught a great many people. And the disciples were first called Christians in Antioch".* (NKJV)

The Bible says the disciples were first called Christians in Antioch (an ancient city in Syria, one time capital of the Roman province in Asia): meaning they were not the ones who branded themselves "Christians" but the outsiders, spectators, onlookers and unbelievers. They looked at how the Apostles and other believers in Christ were behaving and conducting themselves, and decided to call them "Christians".

We should not allow the world to use its own parameters to judge our personality, because they do not know who Christ is, or the Holy Ghost, and neither do they know who we really are in Christ. John 14:17 says it all;

> *The Spirit of truth, whom the world cannot receive, because it neither sees Him nor knows Him; but you know Him, for He dwells with you and will be in you"* (NKJV).

You cannot tell the taste of a soup by its look: and like somebody rightly said, "the taste of the pudding is in the eating". Therefore, somebody who is out of the body Christ cannot tell who someone in Christ really is.

By the way, the name was not given in good faith. It was a name given by the Gentiles to ridicule the believers in Christ. Let's see what the Easton's Bible Dictionary has to say about this;

> "The name given by the Greeks or Romans, probably in reproach, to the followers of Jesus. It was first used at Antioch. The name by which the disciples were known

among themselves were, "Brethren", "The faithful", "Elect", "Saints", "Believers"."[1]

Even the Smith's Bible Dictionary makes us to understand that the disciples did not apply the name to themselves, but it was imposed on them by the Gentile world: and would naturally be used with contempt (the feeling that somebody or something is worthless or beneath consideration).

"The disciples, we are told, [Acts 11:26] were first called Christians at Antioch on the Orontes, somewhere about A.D 43. They were known to each other as, and were among themselves called, brethren, [Acts 15:1, 23; 1Corinthians 7:12] disciples, [Acts 9:26; 11:29] believers, [Acts 5:14] saints, [Romans 8:27; 15:25]. The name "Christian," which, in the only other cases where it appears in the New Testament, [Acts 26:28; 1 Peter 4:16] is used contemptuously, could not have been applied by the early disciples to themselves, but was imposed upon them by the Gentile world.[2]

Imagine, this even tells us that the only other two cases where this name appears in the New Testament, it was used contemptuously. The Encarta English dictionary defines contempt as; "Attitude of utter disgust or hatred: a powerful feeling of dislike toward somebody or

---

[1] Easton Bible Dictionary, page 238, eBook version, by Matthew George Easton, published by Thomas Nelson 1897.
[2] Smith's Bible Dictionary, page 180, eBook version, by William Smith, published by Grand Rapids, MI: Christian classics Ethereal library.

something considered to be worthless, inferior, and undeserving of respect"[3]. Can you now understand how the world sees, considers and obviously treats those who go by the name "Christians"? The Holman illustrated Bible Dictionary on its part reveals that it was a name that was used to address a particular group of slaves.[4]

And the disciples, being very much aware of the name that the pagans have labeled on them, could not address themselves by it, talk less of claiming the name to themselves. Apostle Paul, being very present from the first day the Gentile world named them such, did not even for once, in all his writings to the Church, mentioned the word "Christians".

This tells us a lot. It explains that the name was not only given in bad faith, but was as well used to ridicule, reproach, and treat them with contempt. We all know the kind of persecution the disciples and early believers in Christ went through in the Hands of the peoples of the Roman world. The name "Christian" was also part of their major scheme of persecution.

Now tell me, why will a name that connotes and denotes reproach, contempt and ridicule to a people become a world acclaimed and celebrated name by the same people, if not out of gross ignorance?

By the way, what's the etymological meaning of the word "Christian" in the first place?

The word "Christian" comes from the Greek word "Christianos", which means "Follower of Christ", or "Christ-like". And since there is no Hebrew word for Christian, the word "Christ" (from which

---

[3] Microsoft student with Encarta premium 2009 DVD, Encarta dictionaries.Inc.
[4] Holman Illustrated Bible Dictionary, page 284, Revised and Expanded ©2015 by B&H Publishing Group Nashville, Tennesse.

Christian is derived), in Hebrew is "Messiah", which means "The anointed one". So, bringing the two together to make sense in English will read, "follower of the anointed one", or "like the anointed one".

I think the above is the best and most simple definition of the word "Christian". Yet this definition falls short of so many things. It falls short of the description of a believer as pointed out by the scriptures, and lacks the vital ingredients of who a child of God is as revealed in the Bible.

First, we are not followers of Christ. You know, you can follow a thing and are not part of the thing. We are one with Him - not followers. We are joint heirs with Him. We are one person; He is the head of the church and we are His body. These truths are repeated over and over in scriptures. We can't be His followers because we are an integral part of Him.

> *"For we are members of His body, of His flesh and of His bones".* Ephesians 5:30 (NKJV).

This scripture above does not only stress the fact that we are members of His body, but emphasizes the fact that we are members of even His flesh and His bones.

Second, we are not "like Christ" because we are part of Him. We are one with Him. Our relationship with Jesus Christ cannot be compared with even that of identical twins or people. The name Christian (Christ-like or like-Christ) describes that of identical people, and not our relationship with Christ Jesus. Our relationship with Christ goes further than that. We are not identical but "One with

Him". Jesus Himself goes further to explain this union by using the example of the vine in John 15:5.

> *"I am the vine, you are the branches. He who abides in me, and I in him, bears much fruit; for without me you can do nothing".* (NKJV)

This scripture does not say "he who abides WITH ME; but it says he who abides IN ME". The branch of the vine is not like the stem of the vine; rather, the branch is part of the stem of the vine (they both make a whole). Apostle Paul takes it from Jesus to explain the same thing in another way:

> *"For as the body is one and has many members, but all the members of that one body, being many, are one body, so also is Christ.*
>
> *For by one Spirit we were all baptized into one body-- whether Jews or Greeks, whether slaves or free--and have all been made to drink into one Spirit".* 1 Corinthians 12:12&13

This scripture makes us understand that we are an integral part of the person of Jesus Christ. And if so be it - considering that the scriptures cannot lie - we cannot be "Like Him". We all are the body of Christ and each one of us is a particular member of that wholesome body.

It is like the human body, which is made up of trillions of individual cells in a perfect union.

One problem with most of God's children nowadays is that they have not understood their position in scriptures. If Jesus Christ was not made "us" by God, there would have been no legal grounds for Him to die for our sins on the cross. Else, there would have been an argument that a person cannot die for another man's sins; for it is written that *"...the soul that sinneth, it shall die"* Ezekiel 18:4 (KJV). The devil knows this scripture very well, and as well knows that He (Jesus) totally became "us" on the cross, and died our death. God is also a just God who will not penalize somebody for someone else's faults. By this, we understand that God sees us as "one" with Christ.

The doctrine of our oneness with Christ is so important and powerful to the New Testament church that the world will never help our understanding of it by giving us a name that illuminates this truth; but rather will do the opposite.

The importance of names and their meanings are as well so valuable to God that we see numerous events of naming and renaming in scriptures. God did not change the name of Abram to Abraham, Sarai to Sarah, Jacob to Israel, and Simon to Peter for nothing. Names play a major role in revealing, effecting and enforcing our personalities and destinies.

Thus, it is obvious that the name "Christian" has a lot of negative impacts to the body of Christ, following its scriptural weaknesses and pagan origin.

Never a time have we been told that God instructed them to be called "Christians". Neither are we told that God approved the name. Not even themselves sat at one time and said we have adopted a new name by which we should be called. All they called themselves as we saw earlier was "Brethren", "The faithful", "Saints", "Elect", and "Believers".

Therefore, accepting and adopting the name "Christian" does not only go against scriptures, but against the will of God too. And if we start going against the will of God in something as important as what defines our personality, then we should know that we have missed the mark.

The body of Christ cannot and should not be compromised by one imperfect name called "Christians", that connotes a separable relationship of us and Christ Jesus.

I know some people will be smart to say that, "But the word Christian is found in the Bible!" Yes, they are right, but you can fine almost everything in the Bible; the good the bad and the ugly. And the fact that they are found in the Bible does not legitimize them. How many times is the word used in the entire Bible? Just three times: and of the three times, how many times do the pagans and unbelievers used it? Twice. Only once is the word used by one of the Disciples of Christ. The first time we come across the name in the Bible is in Acts 11:26, where unbelievers used it to define the Saints. The second time the word is used in the Bible is in Acts 26:28, where pagan king Agrippa tells Apostle Paul that he almost convinced him to become a Christian. The last place we see the word used in the Bible is in 1 Peter 4:16, where the Apostle Peter says Christians are a group of people who suffer for no crime committed; and that if you find yourself in like manner, you should glorify God because He will vindicate you.

I know the word "Christian" has been in office for long, but that doesn't make it right. And what makes you think the name that was very unpopular among the members of the early church should be the most popular in the church today? Ironically that's what it is now.

With this conclusion, a question is sure to arise, as to what should replace the imperfect name, or what should a child of God be called. We are called several times in scriptures "Sons of God" or "children of God":

> *"Behold, what manner of love the Father hath bestowed upon us, that we should be called the sons of God: therefore the world knoweth us not, because it knew him not."*   1 John3:1 (KJV).

Here again, the Bible is telling us that the world does not know us, because it doesn't know Christ. So if the world doesn't know us, how can they define us appropriately? The Bible clearly says it here that God has lavished us with much love, that we should be called sons of God, or children of God as some translations put it.

Our life in Christ goes beyond any definition of a religion. You cannot equate it with other religions of the world like Buddhism, Hinduism or Islamism.

Children of God should know who they truly are, and not one novice of a stranger trying to tell them their suggestions of who they think they are.

I pray that God should open our hearts and make us understand the implications and pitfalls of the names we answer. But as for God,

He is always ready to change our names to suite our personalities and destinies. May He change the course of our lives by changing our names, as He did to Abraham, Sarah, Israel and Paul in Jesus' name! Amen.

Chapter Two

ALMS GIVING PUBLICITY

IVING OF ALMS AND OTHER acts of charity, in all the major religions of the world, is considered a righteous act. It is a doctrinal practice that is deeply rooted in the New Testament teachings of Christ, and that of the apostles in the early Church.

Simply put, alms refers to charitable donations of money or other assistance given to people in need.

Giving to the needy is a good and Godly practice that must be encouraged by all means possible in the body of Christ. However, the manner at which the Church goes about the giving of alms today is a serious call for concern.

Going further, we will seek to answer the following questions;
- Does the Bible teach about alms giving?
- What does the Bible say about giving of alms; is it good or bad?
- How should alms be given; is there a right or wrong way of giving alms?

- What are the consequences for the giving or not giving of alms?

As simple as these questions may seem, yet their answers will illuminate so many things in relation to this practice.

The Bible does not only teach about alms giving, but sees it as a Holy act that transcends the physical world. We shall elaborate more on this later. Jesus Himself doesn't only teach us about alms giving, but instructs us to do it, and do it rightly.

> *"Beware of practicing your piety before men in order to be seen by them; for then you will have no reward from your Father who is in heaven. Thus, when you give alms, sound no trumpet before you, as the hypocrites do in the synagogues and in the streets, that they may be praised by men. Truly, I say to you, they have received their reward. But when you give alms, do not let your left hand know what your right hand is doing. So that your alms may be in secret; and your Father who sees in secret will reward you."* Matthew 6: 1- 4 (RSV).

We are going against the teachings of Christ in the above scripture every day, because His teachings on alms giving are not appealing, and are very unpopular.

Today, we prefer to keep the cameras rolling while we give to the needy: take selfies of our alms giving activities; attach them to our social media handles on Facebook, whatsapp, Twitter, Instagram, snapchat and others, for the world to see. At times we invite the press to cover our charitable works; interview the recipients about how they feel to receive such aids, and even go as far as paying the press organs to pass it through the screens as many times as possible, for everyone to see.

We have even gone to the level where we don't wait anymore for people to see our charitable works and praise us, but we now extract the praises from the recipients themselves, immediately they receive from us.

But; "why will Jesus say that we should not make a public show of our charitable works: so that our partners will not see what their money is doing, thereby increasing their partnership, which translates into more money in our accounts? Does He not know that making our charitable works public will give us more partners, who will help us reach more of the needy? He should also know that the publicity of our generosity will advertise us into the world, make the ministry popular, and bring in more people into the Church. Does He not also know that it's another strategy of evangelism? How will the people know that they can run to the Church and ask for help in times of need if we don't make our charitable works public? How will our followers, the younger generation, and other men of God follow after this good practice of charity and reciprocate, if they don't see us doing it? We believe we have good intentions for doing what we are doing. What actually matters is our intentions and not our actions."

Hahaha! Our actions reveal our intentions, and our intentions and actions results to our reward. Who you want to reward your giving will determine how you will go about the giving.

Most of our giving have already been rewarded, yet we still stand in wait for another reward that will never come.

I used to think that God rewards all we do; be it good or bad. But I just realized that God doesn't reward everything. One of them is public giving of alms.

> *"So whenever you give to the poor, don't blow a trumpet before you like the hypocrites do in the synagogues and in the streets so that they will be praised by people. **I tell all of you with certainty, they have their full reward!"***   Matthew 6: 2 (ISV).

How secretive must your giving of alms be in order for you to enjoy God's reward for the act?

> *"When you give something to a poor person, keep it a secret. Do not tell even your best friend. Let it be as if your left hand did not know about your right hand's actions. Nobody else will know about what you gave to the person. It will be a secret. God sees things that are secret. And He will give you good things."*
> Matthew 6: 3 -4 (EasyEnglish).

This is a difficult one right? Should your spouse know about it? Is it necessary? What of your Pastor? If your best friend, and your left hand should not know about it, why should any other person know? It has to be a top secret.

Why should something as simple as giving be made a "top secret"? Well, if you desire its reward from heaven, then you have no option than to comply with the demands of the scriptures.

Secret giving is the secret of the abundance of heavenly blessings. So many people are praying for God to bless them, yet they fail to see the easy way to these blessings that is clearly written in the scripture above.

We hate secret giving, yet love open reward. That's just what we have become. But God is not man. His standards are not compromised by who we are.

I challenge you as a man of God, and by the authority of this written word in Matthew 6:3-4, to practice secret giving for just Three months, and see the results.

True gospel is not the recitation of scriptures, but the practice of the written word.

At this level, I will like you to take a pause, and have at least a minute of reflection on all you have ever given, and see how many times you gave in secrecy.

We should as well take note of the fact that giving of alms does not include giving to someone who has the power to give back to us someday: because majority of the giving we see in the world today are geared towards this direction.

Men of God nowadays have become so political in their giving than even some politicians. This reminds me of what one of my former school principal said one day. He said; "if I give you a five thousands bank note, am not giving it for you; am giving it for myself: because I want people to know that I have given you money, which will make me famous as a philanthropist, thereby working in favour of my political ambition".

All the giving you see being done in the world today are done for different reasons and intentions.

If only you can know the intentions of some of the gifts that come to you, then you will reject many. Some of the gifts that come your way are simply baits from the enemies.

I know of so many people who were killed through gifts. Thus, the Bible is not wrong to say that "...he that hates gifts shall live" (Proverbs 15:27). The easiest way to kill people today is through gifts.

Nevertheless, should we stop giving because people use gifts to kill others? No! The fact that a knife is used to kill does not stop us from using it in the kitchen. Galatians 6:9 says, "let us not abate our courage in doing what is right; for in due time we shall reap a reward, if we do not faint" (Weymouth).

Talking about alms giving, it is important for us to know that there is a far greater reward for our genuine works of charity that transcends the physical world, as seen in Luke 12:33.

"Sell your possessions and give alms. Provide yourselves with purses that will never wear out, a treasure inexhaustible in heaven, where no thief can come nor moth consume" (Weymouth).

Is it possible for you to stay here on earth and do savings in heaven? Well there is only one way out for this reality: alms giving. And for the sake of emphasis, this same truth is reiterated in two other scriptures by Jesus himself;

"Do not lay up stores of wealth for yourselves on earth, where the moth and wear-and-tear destroy, and

where thieves break in and steal. But amass wealth for yourselves in heaven, where neither the moth nor wear-and-tear destroys, and where thieves do not break in and steal" Matthew 6:19-20 (Weymouth).

"'If you desire to be perfect', replied Jesus, 'go and sell all that you have, give to the poor, and you shall have wealth in heaven; and come, follow me'." Matthew 19:12 (Weymouth).

From the above scriptures, it is clear that there is only one way whereby one can have treasures in heaven, which is through alms giving. And if this was not true, Jesus wouldn't have talked about it, talk less of laying emphasis on it.

Judging by your true acts of alms giving, do you have treasures in heaven? Are you interested in such incorruptible treasures? Can you now engage in the process of amassing true wealth in heaven through alms giving? God bless you.

Chapter Three

CHURCH WEDDING

WHEN WE TALK ABOUT WEDDING, we are talking about a marriage ceremony. Marriage is the union of a man and a woman, instituted by God Himself, for the purpose of companionship and procreation. I know there are many kinds of marriages today, and many reasons or purposes why people get married. We now hear of gay or same sex marriages, traditional marriages, court marriages, church marriages, contract marriages, group marriages, and their different forms such as monogamy, bigamy, polygamy, and polyandry. Today, people are even getting married to animals. But no matter how man deviates from the main thing, the facts remain the same; that He who made them from the beginning made them male and female.

It will sound strange to so many to hear that church wedding is an error in the New Testament church. Again, we will move gradually to prove it.

First of all, nothing like "church wedding" ought to exist. A wedding is not a religious nor a church occasion. Nothing like this existed in both the Old and New Testaments. All the weddings we read of in the Bible were never church weddings or religious ceremonies.

Let me begin by quoting the definition of "wedding" from the Zondervan Pictorial Bible Dictionary, which says a "Wedding, is not a religious ceremony..."[5]

The wedding at Cana itself in John 2:1-11 was not a religious or church wedding. It was a traditional wedding. How do we know that? From the location (it took place not in the Temple or a Synagogue), and the ceremony itself (which was celebrated according to the tradition of the people).

Never a day was a wedding contracted in the Temple or Synagogues, as far as the whole Bible is concern. If you care, you can read from Genesis to Revelation, and you will see no such thing.

Now, let's look at the entire Church Wedding setup:

THE VEIL

There are so many wrong things associated with the church wedding. We will begin with the veil. The veil the woman puts on is a symbol of prostitution. It is a Jewish tradition that prostitutes do cover their faces with veils, in order to conceal their evil intentions,

---

[5] Zondervan Pictorial Bible Dictionary, page 889, by Tenny and Merril, published by Grand Rapids, Zondervan Pub. House, 1963.

and hide their faces from the public, as a result of their shameful acts. We see this in the story of Judah and Tamar.

> *"Now in process of time the daughter of Shuah Judah's wife died; and Judah was comforted, and went up to his sheepshearers at Timnah, he and his friend Hirah the Adullamite. And it was told Tamar, saying, "Look, your father – in – law is going up to Timnah to shear his sheep. So she took off her widow's garments, covered herself with a veil and wrapped herself, and sat in an open place which was on the way to Timnah; for she saw that shelah was grown, and she was not given to him as a wife. When Judah saw her, he thought she was a harlot, because she had covered her face. Then he turned to her by the way, and said, "Please let me come in to you"; for he did not know that she was his daughter – in – law. So she said, "What will you give me, that you may come in to me?"* Genesis 38:12-16 (NKJV)

The Bible says when Judah saw her, he took her for a harlot because she had covered her face. This tells us that they were acquainted of harlots in such attire. Tamar herself knew very well that was the attire of the harlot, before going in for it, which of course gave her hundred percent success in her game of deception.

The bride who covers her face with a veil is telling the groom that I am a harlot: and the man who is presented with a veiled lady takes her for a harlot, in relation to this text.

The significance of everything we do matters. For before you know it, an invisible force must have caused you to do and fulfill that which is said and believed of the veil.

The veil is also a tool and symbol of deception. Tamar used but a veil to deceive Judah to go to bed with her. Jacob was deceived by the uncle Laban, to get married to the one he did not love by the use of a veil. The veil was not only used to deceive Jacob into marriage, but also to trick him into another seven years of Labor. Imagine what evil weapon you are dealing with! There is a force of deception and trickery that is behind every veil.

A woman may not understand why she has started telling lies, deceiving and tricking the husband; even though she made up her mind to be true to the man before marriage. It is obvious that the power of the veil is in action.

The issue of the veil stems from a pagan practice and tradition. Laban was a pagan, who worshipped idols. We see this in Genesis 31:32, where Rachel stole the gods of her father. Laban never worshipped the God of Abraham, and neither did his household. He believed in the gods of the pagan tribe of Haran and worshipped them. We see the practice of the veil more than once from his household. He used the veil on Leah and probably on Rachel, the wives of Jacob. Before then, his sister, Rebecca, the wife of Isaac, had used the veil on herself when she was being given out to Isaac (Genesis 24:65). This reveals that the practice of the veil did not begin with Leah and Rachel, but far behind them.

Those who believe in the use of the veil today in marriage quote the situation of Leah, Rachel and Rebecca, referring to this pagan practice of Laban's household. How sad to know that this pagan practice and tradition of Laban's household has gotten a firm root in the New Testament church of Christ!

The veil has a very negative significance and impression in the New Testament. Paul the Apostle wrote that the gods of this world has veiled the faces of many, that they should not see the glory of God and be saved. Thus, wherever we talk of the veil in the New Testament, we talk of a covering of the face and an impediment to vision. How I wish people should understand this and seize from such negative practices.

> *"But their minds were blinded. For until this day the same veil remains unlifted in the reading of the Old Testament, because the veil is taken away in Christ."*
> *2 Corinthians 3:14 (NKJV)*

The veil is used to signify so many negative things. Jesus came to liberate us not only from the power of sin, but from that of the veil as well. The veil is that which separated man from the very presence of God. The most Holy Place at the Temple or Tabernacle (which carried the very presence of God), was separated by a veil (Leviticus 16:2). It acted as a blockage, hindrance or barrier to free access into God's presence. Though it was the sins of the people that brought the veil between them and God, it doesn't cancel the fact that the veil was used as a tool to separate them from their God. The veil stood before them as a reminder of their unworthiness and sinfulness. We see that the veil was actually a problem, when Jesus on the cross, had to destroy and take it away from the people, by tearing it at the Temple from top to bottom (Mathew 27:51). Yet, the veil and its evil memories that Jesus took away is still being brought back to the church today through weddings.

The veil also signifies a covering of glory. When Moses came down from Mount Sinai after spending forty (40) days and nights of fasting and communing with God, his face started shining and radiating so much light (which was the glory of God on him), and the children of Israel could not look at his face (Exodus 34:29-34). He had to cover his face with a veil, before he could speak to them: but whenever he went before God, he removed the veil.

A woman who covers a veil covers the beauty of her face which is a form of the glory of God on her. The glory of God is not to be covered, but to be left open that all might see and praise the God of heaven. Neither do men light a lamp and put it under a table, but on the table; so that it should give light to all that are in the house.

Some people may be saying in their minds that, "But the veil today is not the same as the ones of old in Bible days". Yes, you're right, but what is it called? And is it not still being used in similar occasions? If it's still bearing the same name and performing the same function, then nothing has truly changed.

The believe that the veil is a symbol of virginity, or of testimony that she has not known the man before marriage is a man–made believe; which cannot be proven from the Bible. The Bible does not tell us that the main reason they were putting on the veil was because they had not known men. Tamar who used the veil against Judah was not a virgin. The veil on Moses' face too did not connote virginity. To modify and compromise the word of God for our selfish gains is a very dangerous adventure.

Recently, I heard my wife telling our second daughter, Zoe, that "They don't cover the face: when you cover the face, you become a masquerade; because we don't have dresses (clothes) made to be worn on the face on regular occasions". She was saying so because the child was covering a dress on her face. I followed all what she said with a keen interest, and nodded my head in agreement. Truly we don't have to cover the face, so that we can see clearly where we are going to, and what is ahead of us. Why dress a woman like a masquerade on one of the best days of her life? Why must it be only the woman?

THE VOWS

The marriage vows we swear are also evils that are associated with church weddings. They are against scriptures and the very teachings of Christ. The words; "vow", swear", "pledge", "oath" all mean the same thing, because they are synonyms. If you doubt me, go to the dictionary. Jesus was not a fool to stress on the fact that we should not swear at all.

> *"Again you have heard that it was said to them of old time, 'you shall not make false vows, but shall perform to the Lord your vows,' but I tell you, don't swear at all: neither by heaven, for it is the throne of God; nor by the earth, for it is the footstool of His feet; nor by Jerusalem, for it is the city of the great king. Neither shall you swear by your head, for you can't make one hair white or black. But let your 'Yes' be 'Yes' and 'No' be*

'No'. Whatever is more than these is of the evil one"
Matthew 5:33-37 (WEB).

Anything that causes you to swear is not from God, but from the evil one. You should not swear at all or whatsoever; says the Word of God. Your communication should be simple. if Christ Jesus who is the head of the church is teaching against vows and swearing, and a believer comes to vow, pledge or swear in His church, that person is doing nothing less than an out-right disobedience to the Word of God, and a slap on the face of Christ.

Just the fact that it is called, titled or captioned "marriage vows", is enough to make us understand that this has gone beyond the teachings of the New Testament church.

Vows were not pronounced at the marriages we see in the scriptures. We are given no hint of their existence in marriage ceremonies. Therefore, if the Bible which is our reference book, and its teachings our perfect example, does not tell us that, where has this practice emerged from?

What are marriage vows? We may be talking about them and somebody is saying "what are they talking about?" marriage vows are solemn promises made by the bride and groom, to strictly adhere to, as long as the marriage lasts. An example of such is;

"in the name of God, I,................., take you,..............., to be my wife/husband, to have and to hold from this day forward, for better, for worse, for richer, for poorer, in sickness and in health, to love and to cherish, until parted by death." [6]

---

[6] https://www.marthastewart.com > traditional wedding vows for your ceremony, 25 Mar 2021.

"The oldest traditional wedding vows can be traced back to the manuals of the medieval church in England, published in 1549."[7] We can now see how this thing got into the church of Christ: more than one thousand five hundred years after the death of Christ, and about five Centuries from today.

Vows violate the Biblical option of divorce on the sole account of infidelity, while imposing penalties on the divorcee. We must make the church understand that the Bible gives room for divorce only on accounts of adultery, while at the same time gives no room for remarriage (except on the case of the same person, or the death of one party). Without this, we make ourselves more rigid in the judgment of divorce than Christ Himself. The church has no right to preach on "no divorce whatsoever", when Christ talks of an exception:

> "I tell you that whoever divorces his wife, **except for sexual immorality,** and marries another, commits adultery; and he who marries her when she is divorced commits adultery". Matthew 19:9(WEB)

This is the doctrine that marriage vows seek to promote. In other words, when you have taken a vow before God to keep a woman and not to divorce her on any account, you block that one chance (for the sake of sexual immorality) that Christ gave you. Which means even if you decide to divorce your adulterous wife to stay unmarried, you will still be at fault before God for not respecting your vow; of which you would have been faultless without the vow.

---

[7] https://www.weddingsido.com.au> the oldest wedding vows, 26 June 2022.

However, the simple act of vowing or swearing is in itself against the strict instructions, doctrines and teachings of Christ. The Old Testament gave room for vowing or swearing and making sure it is fulfilled or redeemed. But Jesus gave a strict instruction that we should **not vow at all**. He is not interested in the fulfillment of vows. What He is interested in is that vows should not be uttered at all.

> *"Again you have heard that it was said to them of old time, "do not make false vows, but fulfil your vows to the Lord." But I tell you, **do not swear at all**: neither by heaven, for it is the throne of God; nor by the earth, for it is the footstool of His feet; nor by Jerusalem, for it is the city of the great king. Neither should you swear by your head, for you cannot make one hair white or black. But let your "yes" be "yes" and your "no" be "no". Whatever is more than these is of the evil one."*
> Matthew 5:33 - 37 (NHEB).

Yet, marriage vows are made right before of the church, to challenge the very teachings of Christ which says we should not vow at all: what a blow does the church give to the very face of Christ!

Despite the fact that a church wedding is not found in the Bible, we are not also instructed by scriptures to practice something called church wedding. It is something that was instituted in the church of Christ by some egoistic men of God of old, and copied by those of today.

THE DRESS CODE

Church weddings are also called "white weddings". This is to tell us that it originated from the white race. It will interest you to know (if you can take your time to trace its origin) that church wedding originated from Britain, so many years back. Obviously, will the traditional style of dressing – the flair fairy tale gown, the gloves, the coat and tie – not tell you where the tradition originated from?

The white wedding dress of the bride was made popular by Queen Victoria in 1840, who choose this instead of the bride's best dress as was the case.[8]

The man, obviously as the British tradition demands, will be in their official British attire of the coat and tie.

This traditional dressing code for the church wedding has been maintained till date. Yet, people are not asking themselves that "But why this particular dressing style?" who said it cannot be changed? Is everybody English that you will be forced to dress like a British man or woman, because you want to celebrate your marriage in church? Why don't we think that Africans should dress African, Asians should dress Asian, Europeans should dress European, and Americans should dress American when it comes to church weddings?

Today, it is believed that the bride should wear only the white color gown; not yellow, blue, red, black, or any other color. This, they say, white connotes innocence and virginal purity on the part of the lady. But we know this is just a man-made belief, and that

---

[8] https://www.almanac.com > why are wedding dresses white? Nov 12 2021.

almost a hundred percent of the ladies who wear the white wedding garments in our churches are not innocent virgins.

Some ladies today will openly tell you they just feel like dying if they don't wear that white gown: obviously because they have seen friends and loved ones wearing it. To them, the church wedding dress has become a matter of competition and a show.

The church wedding dress competition is becoming more and more intense as the days go by among young girls. Today it is all about whose wedding garment is the most expensive, or the sexiest, or the most stylish. That's why some of them now go in for a single day wear that costs several millions.

Why all these for a simple dress? At first, the bride and the groom could keep it very simple by wearing just their best available dresses, no matter the color or style.

Church wedding is not a fundamental doctrinal practice that was passed down to us by Jesus Christ or His disciples. Therefore, it should not be used as the basis or measuring rod for church leadership. In some churches today, if you do not make a church marriage, you cannot be made a leader of the church. Yet the Bible says, "A leader of the church must be blameless, the husband of one wife ..." not "...must make a church marriage".

OTHER ASPECTS

Today, church weddings are used as a means to exploit the celebrants, who happen to be children of God and members of the body of Christ. How dangerous it is to steal from a child of God by tricks. Some men of God do encourage church weddings today at all costs, because of so many hidden reasons. They use it to get rich and swell their pockets, get promotion in ministry, become popular and famous in town, etc.

It is also a show-up for pride to the celebrants. I have even heard several men of God saying that church wedding is the pride of the woman; therefore men should not deprive them of that pride of womanhood. Of course, we know that anything related to pride has enough resistance from God. For God resists the proud, but gives grace to the humble. I am sure we are also aware that pride comes before a fall. Obviously that may be the reason why so many marriages today that I know resulted from church weddings are a failure. Always try to avoid anything that can make you proud.

Church weddings also create room for material competition among members of the body of Christ. Here, I see that we have deviated from the teachings of the Bible, of provoking one another to love, into provoking one another to lust after the mundane things of this world. The more flamboyant, decorative and colorful your wedding is, the more you feel elevated above your peers and competitors.

The cost of running a church wedding today is something that is uncalled for. This issue has discouraged and frustrated so many marriages that would have been booming today. Brothers in church are scared of marriage because of the financial burden the church attaches to it. This is a cause of the frustration of many youths in church, which results to fornication.

There is something today I call "the church wedding syndrome". It is a situation where young girls in church today are not ready to get married out of a church wedding. The first thing they ask any man who approaches them for marriage is "will there be a church wedding? If there will be no church wedding, count me out". It is also a situation where the church leaders may tell you in black and white that "outside a church wedding, your marriage is not considered and recognized in this church". Again, the "church wedding syndrome" can be seen in an association of proud individuals who tell members that "one of our by-laws is that any member of this association who wants to marry must do so with the condition of a church wedding".

In some churches today, when an individual gets married without a colorful wedding in church, members turn to look at him with scorn and treat him as "low class". This has even led to a situation of inferiority complex in those who never organized a church wedding for their marriages. I have even witnessed a situation where a pastor stands to preach that God can never bless the marriage of a certain brother in church, because he did not go for a church wedding.

It has also become an avenue of fund raising; wherein the couples are thinking of making money and other material gains, while the church is also thinking seriously of the gains she will make from it. In other words, we can say the main purpose of church weddings to many is the gains and proceeds. Others see it as an opportunity for great business in terms of their stock, and advertisement of their persons and skills. I have heard a young girl saying, "I have to dress well and look attractive for that wedding ceremony; who knows whether I might have my own man there also?"

The irony of it all is that church wedding has no relevance, significance and importance before God. It is not a church wedding that necessitates God's approval of a marriage nor brings His blessings into the marriage. The moment you pay the dowry of a woman, and her parents and people give her to you, you become legally married before God. And when you continue to do and obey the word of God as concerns marriage, you start harvesting God's blessings in your marriage.

When Jesus made the statement that *"what therefore God has join together, let no man put asunder",* there were no church weddings. That is, weddings by this time were not religious occasions. How therefore could God join something that did not practically include the church? When Jesus said *"for this cause shall a man leave father and mother, and shall cleave to his wife; and the two shall be one flesh,* He did not say they must be cleave together by a pastor or any religious authority, before they can become one flesh.

We should again take note that the wedding at Cana of Galilee in John 2:1-10, where Jesus was an invited guest, was not a religious occasion, and neither did it take place in a church (synagogue or Temple). In fact, Jesus, though fully present with His entourage, was not even called up for a brief sermon or word of prayer. The occasion was strictly traditional.

So, no matter what is done, performed and said in a church wedding ceremony, it is an irrelevant drama of worldliness and ignorance before God. If it's about the preaching, teaching and exaltation, the couple can still be taught and advised out of that ceremony. In fact, they should be taught before even making plans for. Even the prayers for the couple can as well be done out of the ceremony.

Why cause people to borrow and spend so much money for a mere show, and later faint of hunger and lack in the house? I know of people whose financial lives have never been fine since after their wedding. They are still working very hard to meet up with debts, rather than a good living, even after five (5) years in marriage.

Worse of it is that so many abominations that cause desolation are brought into the church today in the name of weddings. Homosexual, lesbian, and other kinds of such abominable marriages are being contracted and celebrated in the church of Christ nowadays.

Nevertheless, if you cannot do without a wedding at all, then it should be a short ceremony of simplicity, with the lady covering no veil and the marriage vows not read. The traditional wedding regalia of the white gown and coat may not even be respected. And after the putting of rings by the couple, the minister may end the occasion with the words, "with the power vested on me, I pronounce you before the congregation of the saints, husband and wife", after which prayers are offered for the two. Though, this too is compromising the standards of the gospel.

I wait to see and know of a pastor today who will encourage the young people only to go for the complete payment of the dowry of their wives, and come for just prayers on them.

Though I am not here to comment on the entire subject of marriage, I will like you to think of an ideal marriage in scriptures. The only one I know of is that of Adam and Eve, keeping aside that of Jesus Christ and the church, to happen in the future. I consider the marriage of Adam and Eve ideal because it is the only marriage that Jesus made reference to in scriptures, and on a positive note for that matter: telling us to look unto it as an example of monogamy and an inseparable union that knew no divorce.

"And he answered and said unto them, have ye not read, that He which made them at the beginning made them male and female, and said, for this cause shall a man leave father and mother, and shall cleave to his wife; and they twain shall be one flesh? Wherefore they are no more twain, but one flesh. What therefore God hath join together, let no man put asunder". Matthew 19:4-6 (KJV).

What we should learn from this marriage are;

The marriage never knew divorce – which was a very serious issue in the Jewish society of the Old Testament up to the time of Jesus – though we may say there was no other woman apart from Eve that Adam would have gotten married to. Yet, he would have still divorced her due to anger and frustration, to stay alone: of course there are many today who have divorced to remain single.

The marriage also knew no adultery – which was a pandemic in Israel up to the days of Jesus. Fidelity ruled their marriage, thanks to the absence of other women.

The marriage knew no quarrelling, considering that we are not told of any, though they had a problem that would have made them quarrel throughout life – the eating of the forbidden fruit.

The marriage enjoyed perfect unity even in error and sin. Nothing was strong enough to break the bond of unity between them. No doubt Jesus had to comment on it; *"… and they twain shall become one flesh … and they are no more twain, but one flesh. What therefore God hath join together, let no man put asunder".*

The marriage had its errors, difficulties and challenges – showing that it was a real down to earth marriage like many today, and not one "perfect" marriage from space that we cannot compare ourselves with.

The marriage type was also the ideal one – not the polygamy, polyandry, contract, bigamy, homosexual, lesbian marriages that we have today.

And my observations are these;

No vows were said and no pledges were made.

No veil was worn and no special dresses considered.

No rings were worn and no bridal train considered.

Chapter Four

SERVANT OF GOD

THE WORD SERVANT, AS DEFINED by the "Oxford Advanced Learner's Dictionary" means; "1. A person who works in somebody else's household for wages and often for food and lodging. 2. A person who performs services for others, especially as an employee of a company or an organization". [9]

The above definition clearly states that the servant works for food, money and shelter. The second states in clear terms also that he is employed; meaning he can be sacked and replaced by another, if he fails to serve well.

The word "Servant" comes from four Greek words; "Diakŏnŏs" as in John 12:26, "Dŏulŏs" as used in John 15:15, "Ŏikĕtĕs" as used in Like 16:13 and "Pais" as used in Luke 7:7; which all mean; errand

---

[9] Oxford Advanced Learner's Dictionary of current English, page 1075, by A S Hornby, Sixth edition, Edited by Sally Wehmeier, published by Oxford University Press.

boy, attendant, waiter at table, slave, bondman, servant, domestic servant, servant to a king, and many similar things.

All these point to the fact that a servant of God is somebody who works for God (his employer) for money, food, shelter and other basic needs. He is not free, as he is bound by certain laws, rules and regulations, and does not have a say or place in the affairs of the family of God. He does not also know the family secrets and is not allowed to come to where the family seats and discuss. He commands no respect and little interest of the family. He works very hard to gain approval, so as to remain in the family and not be replaced by another. He does all the odd jobs and dirty errands of the family and his opinions doesn't count at all when decision making matters are concerned.

In fact, in our key verse below, some Bible translation like the "New living translation" and the "Amplified Bible" talk of slaves in the place of servants as seen in the "King James version". This therefore makes us understand that servants are not different from slaves. That is, servants in other words are slaves. So, if a "servant of God" is called a "slave of God", he should not be annoyed because they all mean the same thing.

If you are a servant or slave to a family, you are not that only to he who employed you (the head of the family), but a slave and servant to even the least member of that family.

I know some people have a different mentality about who a "servant of God" is, and have tried to define it even in books in a way that is not so demoralizing, but the scriptures are very clear concerning this matter:

"Henceforth I call you not servants; for the servant knoweth not what his lord doeth: but I have called you friends; for all things that I have heard of my father I have made known unto you". John 15:15 (KJV)

"I no longer call you slaves, because a master doesn't confide in his slaves. Now you are my friends, since I have told you everything the father told me" John 15:15 (NLT).

As from the date of announcement of these words by Jesus Christ, our status changed, and heaven took note of the change. Yet it has taken us so long to appreciate this change of status. If Jesus Christ can no longer call you a servant, who then is qualified to call you that which God has put a band on?

No matter the compromising explanations and interpretations we may want to give to the above scripture, the words of Jesus stand. So, we should not even dare to cunningly keep ourselves in bondage by giving some flimsy reasons and excuses to back our stand. I am very uncomfortable when somebody calls me a servant of God; even though I may be silent and not react – for reasons that I may not have much time to clarify the person, or I want to avoid some unnecessary Biblical arguments.

In fact, I used to be very pleased some years back by a brother of mine, who will call me "servant of the Most High God", whenever he noticed my appearance. But today, that same title irritates me – because I have known the truth.

God doesn't call us or treat us as servants or slaves anymore; and He does not want us to be called or treated as such by anybody. The earlier we know and accept this, the better.

The fact that a man's children or wife do serve him in one way or the other does not mean they are servants. So, though a child, I can serve God, but that does not make me a servant. Children are never servants in their fathers' houses: likewise wives are never servants in their husbands' houses. And it does happen that we are both children to God and the Bride of Christ.

At the day of Jesus' pronouncement of John 15:15, we graduated from servant hood to friendship with God. Yet, it did not end there! God had more for us. The bigger news is that we did not end at friendship with God, but graduated from friendship to sonship by Christ's death on the cross for our sins and His consequent resurrection from the grave.

When Jesus Christ resurrected from the grave, He gave us a new life, a new status and a new name whereby we should be addressed;

"Wherefore thou art no more a servant, but a son: and if a son, then an heir of God through Christ". Galatians 4:7 (KJV)

"Behold, what manner of love the father hath bestowed upon us, that we should be called the sons and God …" 1 John 3:1-29 (KJV)

"But as many as received Him, to them gave He power to become the sons of God, even to them that believe in His name". John 1:12 (KJV)

"For as many as are led by the Spirit of God, they are the sons of God.

The Spirit Himself beareth witness with our spirit, that we are the children of God.

And if children, then heirs; heirs of God, and joint – heirs. With Christ; if so be that we suffer with him, that we may be also glorified together". Romans 8:14, 16-17 (KJV)

The Bible declares that *"… thou art no more a servant, but a son; …".* Therefore, any person, whether a bishop or archbishop who tries to oppose this declaration by reason of his own human understanding of our relationship with God, except for his ignorance, should be seriously warned.

I understand that some people consider it a form of humbleness and humility before God by addressing themselves His servants. But any humility that reduces you to a fool is no humility.

By the scriptural declaration of Galatians 4:7 and others as seen above, we have been made sons of God, from servant-hood, passing through friendship. Thus, we are no more friends to God but sons. And until you start reasoning and acting like a son of God and not a friend, you will hardly be an heir of His. It is the exclusive right of sons to be heirs.

By reason of these scriptural findings and understanding, we should not be addressed as servants of God, nor friends, but sons of God. Some may say it doesn't matter and neither does it change anything. But it will do us a lot of good; likewise so many things will go wrong if we reject this revelation knowledge pointed to us by Christ Himself, and the Apostles.

Some others may raise a wise argument that Apostle Paul and others, who point out several times in scriptures that we are no more servants but sons to God, introduced themselves – especially at the beginning of their letters – also severally as servants or slaves of God. Here, we should understand that there were times they wrote by reason of their human understanding, thereby struggling to present a humble image of themselves before God by using the wrong expression, and consequently contradicting the divine truth that they might have proclaimed earlier or will proclaim later.

However, we should be able to learn from their errors and see ourselves in the image of the word of God and nothing else. God bless you as you accept these Biblical facts, which are nothing near philosophical arguments as some may think.

Chapter Five

DEDICATION

THE WORD "DEDICATION" IS FROM a host of Hebrew words like Kâdhēsh, hǎnukkâh, chânak and others, which are translated in English to mean;
Sanctify, Consecrate, Initiate, Purify, Disciple, Pronounce holy, Set apart and Sacred.

Dedication therefore in this context, is the act or practice of setting apart somebody or something as sacred (holy) unto God.

Dedication became a law in Israel the day they left Egypt for the promise land. The Lord commanded them through Moses to observe it as a law, as pointed out in verse 9 of Exodus 13.

The Bible tells us that they were commanded to dedicate only first born sons (excluding first born daughters) and first born male animals. This was because the Angel of the Lord passed through Egypt, killing only the first born sons and first born male animals of the Egyptians. They were strictly commanded to observe this law of dedication as a week-long ceremony, during the month of Abib, each year. They were also commanded not to eat yeast or keep it during this one week period. Other instructions like the compulsory redemption of all first-born sons by a lamb or young goat, and the voluntary redemption of first born male animals were given.

> *"And the Lord spoke unto Moses, saying sanctify unto me all first-born, whatsoever openeth the womb among the children of Israel, both of man and of beast: it is mine. And Moses said unto the people, Remember this day, in which ye came out from Egypt, out of the house of bondage; for by strength of hand the LORD brought you out from this place: there shall no leavened bread be eaten. This day came ye out in the month Abib. And He shall bring thee into the Land of the Canaanites, and the Hittites, and the Amorites and the Hivites, and the Jebusites, which He sware unto thy fathers to give thee, a land flowing with milk and honey, that thou shalt keep this service in this month. Seven days thou shalt eat unleavened bread, and in the seventh day shall be a feast to the LORD. Unleavened bread shall be eaten seven days; and there shall no leavened bread be seen with thee, neither shall there be leaven seen with thee in all thy quarters. And thou shalt show thy son in that day, saying, this is done because of that which the LORD did unto me when I came forth out of Egypt. And it shall be for a sign unto thee upon thine hand and for a memorial between thine eyes that the LORD'S law*

may be in thy mouth: for with a strong hand hath the LORD brought thee out of Egypt. Thou shalt therefore keep this ordinance in his season from year to year. And it shall be when the LORD shall bring thee into the land of the Canaanites, as he sware unto thee and to thy fathers, and shalt set apart unto the LORD all that openeth the Matrix, and every firstling that cometh of a beast which thou hast; the male shall be the LORD'S. And every firstlings of an ass thou shalt redeem with a lamb; and if thou wilt not redeem it, then thou shalt break his neck: And all the firstborn of man among thy children shalt thou redeem." Exodus 13:1 – 13 (KJV).

At that time, the law was restricted only to first born sons and first male animals. Later in their walk to the promise land, it was extended to include buildings and other properties.

And the officers shall speak unto the people, saying, what man is there that hath built a new house, and hath not dedicated it? Let him go and return to his house, lest he die in the battle, and another man dedicate it." Deuteronomy 20:5 (KJV).

Though this passage of scripture talks of instilling courage in the hearts of the Israelite soldiers before their enemies, it points out to one important fact, that it was an obligatory aspect for all Israelites to dedicate their new buildings.

Persons and properties dedication in the Old Testament was practiced under the observation of the law: meaning it was a law that people and properties should be dedicated to God. And dedication therefore as a law, had certain procedures and rituals to be observed, as well as punishment meted upon its defaulters.

Among various dedicated things in the Old Testament were; The first born male of man and beast (Exodus 13:1-15)

Private dwellings (Deuteronomy 20:5).

The tabernacle (Numbers 7: 1-11).

The Temple (2 chronicles 7:5).

The city walls (Nehemiah 12:27).

Temple treasures (1 Chronicles 28:12).

Booty of war (1 Chronicles 26:27).

Persons and things were also dedicated to pagan gods. An example is Nebuchadnezzar's image in Daniel 3

> *King Nebuchadnezzar made an image of gold, ninety feet high and nine feet wide, and set it up on the plain of Dura in the province of Babylon. He then summoned the Satraps, the Prefects, Governors, Advisers, Treasures, Judges, Magistrates, and all the other provincial officials*

to come to the dedication of the image he had set up.
Daniel 3:1-2 (NIV).

In John 10:22, we see that the Jews also had a feast called the 'feast of the dedication'; which was a yearly celebration commemorating the cleansing and rededication of the Temple by Judas Maccabaeus, after it was polluted by Antiochus Epiphanes in 167 B.C.

However, our concern here is to elaborate on;

- The fact that dedication is a law that was strictly observed in the Old Testament.
- The fact that dedication is a doctrinal practice that was not passed down to us by Jesus Christ and His disciples.
- The truth that dedication was not taught and neither was its practice advised in the early church.
- The truth that the present day New Testament Church of Christ ought not and should not beyond any reasonable doubt practice dedication, because we are not under the law.
- The fact that the Church can organize special prayers today for people, things and properties, which do not go with the name "dedication" and the observation of its rituals as was the case in the Old Testament.

Seeing dedication therefore in the perspective of a law, if it should be maintained in the New Testament Church of Christ, it should be done as spelt out in the Old Testament:

- Only firstborn sons should be dedicated and not otherwise, with their redemption of a lamb or young goat presented at the alter.
- All our firstborn male animals must be brought to church and dedicated, with their redemption brought to the alter, or the animals killed.
- It should be a week-long feasting at the first month of the Jewish calendar year, without the eating and keeping of bread made with yeast or yeast itself, with regards to all the other commandments attached to the ceremony.
- All our houses and other properties dedicated, else we face the consequences of defaulting: and we all know what it means to default a law.

But, if we are not to observe the law of dedication in the New Testament church, there should be no trace of its existence in the church. There are only two things; either we are into dedication or not. We should stop mixing up things and confusing ourselves.

The irony is that man does not sanctify or purity a vessel for God. Man does not consecrate, initiate, and set apart a fellow man to God; except when the instruction to do so is coming from God Himself. On our own, we lack the divine ability to make clean something or somebody, before the eyes of God. Besides, can man know what is good or not good for God? It is not the prayer that sanctifies, purifies or sets apart but God Himself.

Putting this therefore into consideration, do the men of God today seek to know the will of God before going in for their numerous dedications of people and things? Does God approve of all the dedications we do today in His name? I think under normal circumstances, before going in for any dedication, we should take the matter to God first.

There are so many foreign and invalid doctrines in the church of Christ today, yet, many of God's children have not taken enough time to sort out and differentiate that which is given to them by Jesus Christ as a New Testament doctrine, and that which is man-made doctrine, or carried forward doctrines from the Old Testament to the New, which do not co-relate with the teachings of Christ.

Jesus had to be dedicated because he was a Jewish first born son, and had to pass through all what a Hebrew child ought to go through to be confirmed as a real Jew. This was very necessary for Him and for His teachings to be accepted in Israel. Else, He would have been looked upon as an outcast and somebody not fit to be called a Jew; talk-less allowing Him teach in the synagogues. His dedication was not done with the purpose of it to be an example for every New Testament church to copy. We should not make mistakes about this.

When He became a grown up man and started teaching and laying the foundation of the New Testament doctrines, He never taught on dedication, and neither did He make it a fundamental New Testament doctrine. The doctrine of dedication was not passed down to us by Jesus Christ nor His immediate Apostles. Thus, the big question here is "how comes the New Testament church of today is practicing dedication?"

Dedication was not also taught and neither was it practiced in the early church. I don't even think a person like Apostle Paul, who so much preached against the law could have encouraged dedication in the early church, even in the slightest terms. Dedication was given as a doctrine or law to the Jews to observe and not the Gentiles. Thus, with the coming of the gospel of Jesus Christ to the Gentile world, it could not have been a fundamental doctrine to the Gentile Church of Christ.

The present day New Testament Church ought not and should not beyond any reasonable doubt, practice dedication. In our Churches today, we see female children being dedicated, at any time of the year, without any dedication ritual, or their redemption: which was not so in the Old Testament. While others like animal dedications do not even appear on scene.

Why all this confusion? God is not an author of confusion. Why struggle to give dedication a place it hasn't in the New Testament Church? The Bible clearly tells us not to add nor subtract what we have been given as the word (Revelation 22:19). The earlier we cause certain things to disappear from the church of Christ (that were not there in the first place), the better, because every little thing will be considered on judgment day.

> *"Neither are we justified by the law, but by grace through faith. Instead we have been delivered from the law, that being dead wherein we were held; that we should serve in newness of spirit, and not in the oldness of the letter.* Galatians (KJV).

This tells us that we are not under the dictates of dedication, which is a law by itself. Why go back into something you have been delivered from, like a dog going back to lick up its vomit? I believe we should not make things hard for God in His dealings with us.

To organize special prayers for our children when they are born, our properties when newly bought or houses when newly constructed is not a bad thing. In fact, I personally encourage that. We should actually pray and thank God for everything we get here on earth, before assuming ownership on them. What is wrong is giving that special prayer the name "dedication". There is a particular occasion in the Old Testament that owns the name "dedication". When you are invoking that name upon your occasion, you should be ready and able to bear the consequences that accompany the name. We all know the significances of names and the roles they play on the bearer, as shown to us by the many Biblical examples of Jacob, Abram, Sarai, Jabez, Saul and others.

I have no problem with organizing a special prayer for a particular thing. I only have a problem with organizing an occasion called "dedication" in the New Testament era.

How do you feel after knowing this, when inviting people and telling them to attend the "dedication" of your child, house or car? You can organize prayers for your children or properties, and invite your brethren, the church, your pastor and friends. The issue is, don't call it dedication. You can call it "Presentation".

I know some may argue that, "when we talk of dedication, we are not referring to the dedication of the Old Testament or something like that: we are talking of something very different from that of the Old Testament". But, what do you mean by dedication in the context of the word of God? Is dedication a New Testament doctrine or not? Was there any with that name in the early church of Christ that can stand as an example for us all to follow? Why import doctrines from other religions and plant them in the church of Christ.

Dedication, like any other law, has a curse or penalty attached to it. And anyone who goes to practice it is directly or indirectly under a curse, if he doesn't do it rightly: "for as many as are of the works of the law are under the curse: for it is written, curse is everyone that continued not in all things which are written in the Book of the law to do them" (Galatians 3:10).

Chapter Six

MYSTERIOUS GOD

THE WORD MYSTERIOUS MEANS; "1. Unknown: about whom or which little is known, but who or which excites considerable curiosity. 2. Strange: difficult to understand or explain. 3. Full of mystery: full of or suggesting mystery. 4. Secretive: deliberately arousing curiosity by refusing to reveal something."[10]

Therefore, if we are talking of a mysterious God, we mean a God you can't know or understand; you can't tell His origin; you don't see Him; His deeds are mind blowing and everything about Him is just amazing and difficult to explain.

This is the image that so many children of God have in their minds about their heavenly Father. And this is what they have been professing and confessing all their lives. They have even taught the same and passed on this knowledge to the upcoming generations.

---

[10] Microsoft student with Encarta premium 2009 DVD, Encarta dictionaries.Inc.

Obviously, it is sad to hear a child confessing that about his father. It is indeed pathetic to hear a child saying he doesn't know the father, can't tell the father's origin, can't understand the father, and even his deed are most of the time living him in confusion and doubts. Consequently, that child can't flow well with the father as far as father-child relationship is concern. This is because he can't tell how the father is going to react towards what he will say or do most of the times. Thus, the child is left in a situation of doubt and uncertainty. And a child who doesn't know the father's origin doesn't know his as well.

The Church has been characterized with doubts and uncertainties through the years because of the lack of this understanding of their Father who is in heaven.

Nevertheless, one of the purposes of this work is to demystify God and disarm that incumbent feeling of doubt and uncertainty about His personality in the body of Christ, which is the church.

God is mysterious to those who do not know Him. They can't also understand Him and can't tell of His personality, nor anything that has to do with Him and His actions. They are the ones who should doubt this God, and marvel at His deeds. This is because they are of the world; they don't know Him and can't see Him.

> *"Even the spirit of truth: whom the world cannot receive, because it seeth Him not, neither knoweth Him: but <u>ye know Him</u>; for He dwelleth with you and shall be in you"* John 14:17 (KJV).

God can't hide Himself from His children. And through the years He has been revealing Himself in diverse ways, all in a bid to make His children have a rich knowledge of His person. If God is indeed hiding Himself from His children, then what type of a Father is He? Also, it's only a complete fool of a child who will be living with the father and doesn't know him. A true child of God knows God. The above scripture tells us that.

Jesus also declares in verse 7 of that same John 14 that;

> "If ye had known me, ye should have known my father also: and from henceforth <u>Ye Know Him</u>, and <u>have seen Him</u>" (KJV).

Apostle John again tells us that we know the father when he declares; "I write unto you, fathers, because <u>you have known Him</u> that is from the beginning. I write unto you, young men, because you have overcome the wicked one. I write unto you, little children, because <u>you have known the Father</u>. I have written unto you, fathers, because <u>you have known Him</u> that is from the beginning" 1 John 2:13-14 (KJV).

If there is any child of God confessing that he doesn't know the Father, it means he doesn't know Jesus nor the Holy Spirit. Thus, such is not worthy to be called a child of God.

The doctrine of "no man can see God and live" is rooted in what God told Moses in Exodus 33:20, that "...you cannot see my face; for no man shall see me and live", when Moses asked God to show him His glory. However, this belief had been existing among God's people long before Moses' encounter with Him in the scripture above.

We see this to be true with Jacob, who was excited about having an encounter with God, when he said, "For I have seen God face to face, and my life is preserved" (Genesis 32:30).

Nevertheless, what God actually meant in Exodus 33:20 is that no one can see His face literally and live, but not His person. You will bear with me that the proceeding verses of that same Exodus 33 reveal that God showed Moses all His physical features, except His face.

> "And the LORD said, here is a place by me, and you shall stand on the rock. So it shall be, while My glory passes by, that I will put you in the cleft of the rock, and will cover you with My hand while I pass by. Then I will take away My hand, and you shall see My back; but My face shall not be seen". Exodus 33:21-23 (NKJV)

So, though Moses did not see God's face, can we say unequivocally that Moses did not see God? No! This fact is buttress by other scriptures that tell us of people who saw God, though they too did not see His face. An example of such is found in Exodus 24:10-11.

> "There they saw the God of Israel. Under His feet there seem to be a surface of brilliant blue lapis lazuli, as clear as the sky itself. And though these nobles of Israel gazed upon God, He did not destroy them. In fact, they ate a covenant meal, eating and drinking in His presence" (NLT).

The above scripture emphasizes the fact that the elders of Israel saw God; God Himself, and nothing happened to them. Though this scripture doesn't give us any glimpse of them seeing God's face, yet it is clear that they saw God's downward parts; and the floor on which His feet were standing is vividly described.

One thing that makes me like the above mentioned verses of the Bible so much is that, they state in clear terms that the elders of Israel saw God and nothing happened to them (God did not lay His hands on them, and neither was He annoyed with them in any way); meaning God revealed Himself to them on purpose. The phrases "...they saw God..." and "...gazed upon God..." are written for the sake of emphasis. In fact, they tell us that these nobles did not only have a chat with God, but ate and drank with Him present.

What are we then saying? Is the Bible contradicting itself? Not at all! What the Bible is saying here is that, you cannot see God's literal face, but you can see His other body parts, His person, and His personal manifestations: and that will still mean you have undoubtedly seen Him.

I will like us to understand that it is not like God is just unwilling to show us His face, or He enjoys playing hide and seek with man as far as His true face being revealed is concern. No! He has concealed His face from us for our own good, because our frail human nature cannot withstand the power of His true facial revelation. How do I know this? His discursion with Moses in Exodus 33:17-23 gives me this understanding. Moses enjoyed a very personal and intimate relationship with God, to the extent that there was nothing God would have hidden from him. Secondly, for God to tell Moses that I am going to pass in front of you, for you to see my literal features, but I will use my hand to cover your face so that you don't see my face, and when my face has passed from you, I will remove my hand from your face, so that you can see my back parts, tells us it was not a big deal for God to let Moses see everything. It is only that Moses' human nature could not withstand God's true facial expression. So, that's why while embarking on the adventure of revealing His true nature to Moses, He had to make sure He protects him from being destroyed in the process.

This again tells us that God is very willing and ready to reveal Himself to His beloved children, and doesn't hide Himself from them in any way.

Apart from Moses, the elders of Israel, and Jacob, there are some few people also in the Old Testament who had the opportunity to see God, meet with Him and have a chat with Him. One of such people is Abraham. I am not talking of an Angel sent from God to represent Him, but God Himself. Here is the account we are presented with;

> *"And the LORD appeared unto him in the plains of Mamre; and he sat in the tent door in the heat of the day; And he lift up his eyes and looked and, lo three men stood by Him; and when he saw them, he ran to meet them from the tent door, and bowed himself toward the ground, And said, My Lord, if now I have found favor in thy sight, pass not away, I pray thee, from thy servant: … And the LORD said, shall I hide from Abraham that thing which I do; seeing that Abraham shall surely become a great and mighty nation, and all*

*the nations of the earth shall be blessed in him? For I
know him, that he will command his children and his
household after him, and they shall keep the way of the
LORD, to do justice and judgment; that the LORD
may bring upon Abraham that which he hath spoken
of him. And the LORD said, because the cry of Sodom
and Gomorrah is great, and because their sin is very
grievous ..."*   Genesis 18:1 & 17-20 (KJV)

We know very well that the scriptures do not lie. If it would
have been an Angel sent to represent God, we would not have read
"And the LORD said ..." with the word Lord in capital letters. The
translators knew it was God before they could use capital letters for
the word Lord. Abraham also knew that it was God Himself before
he could address Him as "... the judge of the earth ..." in verse 25.

And at the end of their discussion, God left and we are told in
Genesis 19:1 that the other two persons who accompanied God on
the journey were Angels.

The manner in which Abraham comported himself during their
conversation and the way he carefully choose his words reveals he
was not just talking with any kind of person but with God Himself.
Going through Genesis 18, we see that the phrase "And the LORD
said..." is used severally to emphasize the fact that Abraham did
not only see God but had a chat with Him in the physical realm.

Also, we did not read of three (3) Angels when they came to
Abraham's house (tent). The Bible is clear to make this distinction
because they were not all Angels.

Secondly, the word LORD used in these verses of scripture is translated from the Hebrew word YAWEH which is used to describe only God Almighty.

With all these, we can confidently conclude that Abraham saw God (in His human form) and spoke with Him, and lived many years after that encounter.

Another person in The Old Testament who also saw God was Isaiah the prophet. The Bible records the following in Isaiah 6

> "In the year that king Uzziah died, I saw the Lord sitting upon a throne, high and lifted up, and His train filled the temple. Then said I, woe is me! For I am undone, because I am a man of unclean lips, and I dwell in the midst of a people of unclean lips: for mine eyes have seen the King, the LORD of hosts". Isaiah 6:1$5 (KJV).

Although Isaiah was certainly in the spirit when he saw the LORD and not in the physical as the case of Abraham was, it does not cancel the fact that it was God Almighty he saw. This is because his account of God sitting on His throne, with Seraphim and cherubim having six wings around the throne, shouting Holy, holy, holy, is the LORD..., is very similar with John's account in Revelation 4:7-8.

Here again, the word LORD, which is all in capital letters is translated from the Hebrew, YAWEH, that is used to describe only God Almighty.

Isaiah also, did not only see the Lord but had a chat with Him as well.

So far, we have seen the cases of more than two persons in the Old Testament who saw God and lived. Before we go to the New Testament, I will like to clear out something.

Seeing God does not mean only seeing Him physically. And you must not think that when God wants to reveal Himself to you, you will only see Him in some strange, giant and mysterious form.

Up till date, those who still have the physical and spiritual appearance of Christ, do see God in His fullness.

The account of John the Divine, in the pages of the book of Revelation is what crowns this subject. This is because his account is both detailed and descriptive. He is not only another man who saw God, but a man through whom we see God. Reading his rich descriptive account of his visions of God is seeing God in His full glory.

When Jesus came, He had a stern argument with Philip (one of His disciple) on this subject.

"If you really knew me, you would know my Father as well. From now on, you do know Him and have seen Him." Philip said, 'Lord, show us the Father and that will be enough for us'. Jesus answered: "don't you know me, Philip, even after I have been among you such a long time? Anyone who has seen me has seen the Father. How can you say, 'show us the Father'? Don't you believe that I am in the Father, and that the Father is in me? The words I say to you are not just my own.

Rather, it is the Father, living in me, who is doing His work. Believe me when I say I am in the Father and the Father is in me; or at least believe on the evidence of the miracles themselves. John 14:7-11 (NIV).

Jesus' argument with Philip was based on the fact that anyone who has seen Him (Jesus Christ) has seen the Father. Therefore, we can say that anyone who saw Jesus saw God. This is what Jesus meant. And it is true because the Bible declares that, "for in him dwells all the fullness of the Godhead bodily" Col. 2:9 (NKJV). Jesus was the bodily presentation of the Godhead to the world. Thus, any person who saw Jesus saw God the father, God the son, and God the Holy Spirit in their bodily form and image.

See what the letter of an Apostle to the Hebrews has to say about this matter:

"God, who at various times and in various ways spoke in times past to the fathers by the prophets, has in these last days spoken unto us by His son, whom He has appointed heir of all things, through whom also He made the worlds; who being the brightness of His glory <u>and the express image of His person,</u> and upholding all things by the word of His power, when He had by Himself purged our sins, sat down on the right hand of the majesty on high" Hebrew 1:1-3 (NKJV).

Here, the Bible presents Jesus Christ as the "express image of God's person" and the "brightness of His glory". By saying Jesus is the express image of God; the Bible is telling us that He is the exact, perfect, complete, and undoubtedly the true image of God.

Consequently, the argument that no one has seen God, doesn't make much sense today. Anyone who has seen Jesus Christ has seen God in His Bodily form.

God is not mysterious to His children as far as His image – which is seen in Christ and in the scriptures is concerned.

God is also not mysterious to His own as concerns His origin. He declares to them that "I am the beginning and the end", "the Alpha and Omega", "the Author and finisher ..." "the first and the last".

A reasonable person will understand that if somebody says he is the beginning, it means he began before everything and everything began from him. That is, God began before the beginning of the world as recorded in Genesis chapter one. And if somebody says he is the "first", we should know that all other persons and things began from him and after him. So, it will be foolish to ask of his mother or father or creator, else they would have been the first before him.

Any child of God who does not understand God does not have the Holy Spirit, and therefore is not worthy to be called one. This is because the Bible says the Holy Spirit is the one who reveals the truth about the Father to us: "However, when He, the Spirit of truth, has come, He will guide you into all truth; for He will not speak of His own authority, but whatever He hears He will speak; and He will tell you things to come" John 16:13 (NKJV). And I also believe the Bible is there to make us understand who God was, is, and will forever be. Thus, any believer in Christ who doesn't understand God has not read the scriptures enough to know at least how He operates.

He went further to say He has not ask them to seek Him in Vain – meaning those who seek Him will find Him: "And you will seek me and find me, when you search for me with all your heart"

Jeremiah 29:13 (NKJV). Here, He did not present Himself as an unreachable God; and never made Himself nor His word mystical to His children, and never has it being His intention to do so. Therefore, His children should stop mystifying Him.

With the help of the Holy Spirit, we have a rich understanding of the Bible. And with this understanding, we get to know God. It becomes therefore erroneous for us to say that God is mysterious.

God makes His secrets known to His children: "The Lord tells His secrets to those who respect Him; He tells them about His agreement" Psalm 25:14 (NCV). And so has it been right from the time of the patriarchs like Abraham, and it cannot stop now. He has already made us to know even the future;

- The end of the world (Matthew 24:1-51).
- Rapture (1 Thessalonians 4:15-17; 2 Thessalonians 2:1-12).
- Judgment (Revelation 20:11-15).
- Heaven (Revelation 21:1-27).
- Hell (Luke 16:19-31).

Every other thing that should be known, has been made known by God. God is not secretive when it comes to His children. The only thing is that some of His children have rejected wisdom, knowledge and understanding, and are not able to fathom all that is written in the Holy Book.

God is not a mysterious being who cannot be reached, known or understood. He knows His children, and they also know Him. When He acts, they know, and when He speaks, they know He is the one speaking. That is why Jesus is bold to declare that;

"I am the good shepherd; I know my own sheep, and they know me... My sheep listen to my voice; and I know them, and they follow me". John 10:14, 27 (NLT).

From today, I charge you (if truly you are a child of God) to stop calling God a mysterious Father, I don't think even God is happy with that. You should also stop singing that "God works in mysterious ways". He is not what you may think and can never be brought low to the level of our carnal thoughts.

Chapter Seven

THE THEORY OF ADOPTION

THE WORD OF GOD IS preached with a lot of illustrations and figures of speech, to help explain spiritual things to physical men. We see this even in the teachings of Jesus Christ when He says: "the kingdom of heaven is like this..." or "the kingdom of God is like unto…"

An illustration helps to portray reality, but is never the true image of reality. Therefore, Apostle Paul like many others use illustrations, metaphors and figures of speech to help drive in the gospel of the kingdom into the hearts of men.

The theory of adoption is one of those illustrative tools that Apostle Paul uses to help us understand our position as sons of God. However, like any other illustration, it falls short of the reality.

The word adoption is from a Greek word; "huiothesia", which means "the placing as a son" in English. It is practiced by the Hebrews in two major ways: one of which is the legal transfer of ownership of a son from one parent (s) (in most cases the biological parents) to another (the adopting parent(s)). In this case, the adopted son is considered like a son born in the family. He can no longer inherit from his natural father. So far as his former family is concern, he is dead.

An adopted child could also be bought over from his/her natural parent(s).

The adopted child becomes a member of the adopting parent(s) by legal procedures and not by natural birth: meaning that he does not possess the D.N.A/RNA of the new parent(s), though he has the legal and moral freedom to act like any other child (if there be any) of the adopting parent(s).

The second practice of adoption is seen when a Hebrew son grows from a Teknon (baby son) to a Teknion (young boy) and finally to a Huios (mature son) and is presented to the public by his natural parents through a party called the "feast of adoption". During this feast, the father of the son makes a public declaration of the son as now being recognized as a mature son of that house. That is, it is a public declaration that goes with the graduation of the son from boyhood to manhood. The boy's father is therefore saying that I now have a child I can call my son (huios).

A scriptural example of this public declaration can be seen in Matthew 3:17, where God declares Jesus in public: *"...saying, this is my beloved son in whom I am well pleased"*. The Greek word used in this scripture in the place of son is "huios".

The word huiothesia (adoption) is used by Apostle Paul to describe our relationship with God in a triple significant capacity, which is as follows;

 – We have been adopted by God by being bought with a price.

- We have been adopted by God, from the kingdom of darkness into His marvelous light, through legal procedures
- We have been adopted (publicly declared as mature sons of God) in Christ, through His own adoption or public declaration in Matthew 3:17.

However, this theoretical illustration of our relationship with God by Paul the Apostle, has its weaknesses like any other illustration, because we have not just been "adopted" by God, but we are "born" of Him by His word through the death and resurrection of Jesus Christ our Lord. For it is written;

> "But as many as received Him, to them gave He power to become _sons of God_, even to them that believe on His name: which were _born_, not of blood, nor of the will of the flesh, nor of the will of man, _but of God_".
> John 1:12-13 (KJV).

The divine truth is that we are born of God and not adopted by God. It is also written; _"Of His own will begat He us with the word of truth, that we should be a kind of first fruits of His creatures"_ James 1:18 (KJV). I will also like us to read what the Amplified version of the Bible states of this verse. _"And it was of His own (free) will that He gave us birth (as sons) by (His) word of truth, so that we should be a kind of first fruits of his creatures (a sample of what He created to be consecrated to Himself)"_ James 1:18 (Amp).

The two scriptures above clearly states that we are "born of God", not by blood, nor by the will of man, nor by the will of the flesh, but by God. That is to say our birth into the family of God is not physical, but spiritual. If God is Spirit, and we relate to Him in the spirit, it is therefore right for us to say we are born spiritually into the family of God, than to say we are adopted spiritually into the family of God. The Bible says, "Jesus answered, 'I tell you the truth, no one can enter the kingdom of God unless he is born of water and of the Spirit. Flesh gives birth to flesh, but the Spirit gives birth to spirit.'" John 3:5-6 (NIV). Here, we see that the only way of belonging into God's kingdom and family is by birth, and not by adoption.

Apostle Paul's theoretical illustrations of us being bought or being adopted by God helps us to understand our position in God's holy family, and not our person. Our person will have to do with our spiritual composition: which will bring our D.N.A/R.N.A in relation to God on stage. As far as our person in relation to God is concern, the Bible stresses on a very serious note that we have been born of God. The proof that we are born of God is that we carry the D.N.A of God, which is His Spirit (the Holy Spirit); whereby we cry, Abba father.This means that we have Zoē (eternal life or the God kind of life) in us.

> "And this is the record that God hath given us eternal
> life, and this life is in His son"   1 John 5:11(KJV)

Apostle Paul's theoretical illustrations of us being bought and adopted by God are not wrong, and were not used wrongly; becaiuse he used them as tools to drive in the real message: but has been mistaken by contemporary gospel preachers and Bible students, to define our personal relationship with God. Yet it is sweet to know the truth; and this is what you have just discovered.

There is something about being born of God that Jesus came to demystify. He told Nicodemus in John 3:3 that *"... except a man be born again, he cannot see the kingdom of God"*. The stress is not on being bought with a price or being adopted or redeemed; the stress is on being born anew. You can be bought with a price, adopted, redeemed, but when you are not born again, you cannot (the Amplified puts it nicely: "...cannot [ever]...") see the kingdom of God. Three strong words used repeatedly in this John 3:3-7, helps us understand where the stress is;

- **Except** – used in verse 3 and 5.
- **Must** – used in verse 7 and
- **Cannot** – used in verse 3 and 5.

Let us take the reading of this passage of scripture all over again, while taking note of the areas of emphasis.

> *"Jesus answered and said unto him, verily, verily, I say unto thee, <u>except</u> a man be born again, he <u>cannot</u> see the Kingdom of God. Nicodemus saith unto him, How can a man be born when he is old? Can he enter the second time into his mother's womb, and be born?*
>
> *Jesus answered, verily, verily, I say unto thee, <u>Except</u> a man be born of water and of the Spirit, he <u>cannot</u> enter into the kingdom of God.*

That which is born of the flesh is flesh; and that which is born of the Spirit is spirit.

Marvel not that I said unto thee, ye <u>must </u>be born again" John 3:3-7 (KJV).

I have come to understand that we have been preaching everyday on being born again without fully understanding what it actually means to be born again.

The Greek word for "born" in this scripture (John 3:3) is "gĕnaō, ghen-nahó" with "procreate" as its English equivalent: meaning God gives birth to us when we are born again, as physical parents give birth to physical children. That is, God multiplies Himself spiritually in the same way man does physically. The only difference between the two is that one is physical while the other is spiritual. The same Greek word (gĕnaō) that is used in John 3:3-8 to explain our spiritual birth is also used in other scriptures like John 9:19 and Luke 1:57 to explain our physical birth.

This teaching of Christ was a difficult one to Nicodemus, and likewise many in today's church. Jesus explains that "that which is born of the flesh is flesh (a different thing) and that which is born of the Spirit is spirit (another thing altogether) of a common process. He was saying in simple terms that "as man replicates himself through physical birth, so too does God replicates Himself through spiritual birth. That is why it is written for our understanding that, *"I have said, ye are gods; and all of you are children of the Most High"* Psalm 82:6.

Jesus goes further to explain in the above passage that when you are born of the Spirit, you are spirit: and when you are born of the flesh, you are flesh. Paul understood clearly this teaching of Jesus, before he could write Romans 8:9 *"but you are not in the flesh, but in the spirit ..."* He spoke so many things about being in the spirit, walking in the spirit and living a spiritual life, because he understood fully well the teaching of being born again.

We are spirits, because we are born by the Spirit. To be born again means to become a spirit, through birth by the Spirit. A man who is born by the Spirit is controlled by the Spirit and not the flesh. It took me several years to understand this teaching of us being spirits. But now, I understand exactly what Apostle Paul means when he says *"therefore, if any man be in Christ, he is a new creature: old things are passed away; behold, all things are become new"* 11 Cor. 5:17. The new creature here is a spiritual creature and not a physical one.

To be born again means to become a spiritual child of God (taking into consideration that God has no Physical children), and therefore a god. If the people of the world can understand this, they will not hesitate to be born again. I am not talking of going to Church. Nicodemus was a religious leader, but Jesus told him to be born again.

Chapter Eight

BLOOD OF JESUS MISUSE

WHEN WE TALK OF THE blood of Jesus, we are referring to that red fluid (plasma) that flowed through the body of Jesus Christ when He was on earth, before His death on the cross.

This blood, which dripped on the surface of the earth from His body, while He was being beaten during the crucifixion, is of great spiritual value and significance to the children of God: owing to the fact that the blood was without corruption – since He was not conceived through sexual intercourse, but was formed by God Himself in the womb of a virgin – and was shed for many reasons.

It is owning to these multiple reasons that the body of Christ, which is the church, has begun using the blood of Jesus Christ for purposes that do not correspond with the word of God as written in the Bible concerning that blood.

Notwithstanding, we will in this chapter, try to redress the situation that is plaguing the church in this area of the blood. But before we do that, we will out – line the various ways and purposes by which the Bible tells us the blood of Jesus is meant for.

The blood of Jesus Christ is meant for the remission of sins. *"Whom God had set forth to be a propitiation through faith in his blood, to declare his righteousness for the remission of sins that are past, through the forbearance of God",* Romans 3:25. That is, the canceling of a debt, prison sentence or decree of pain and disease. This remission effected by the blood of Christ comes into force when a sinner accepts Jesus Christ as his personal Lord and Savior.

The second scriptural use of the blood of Jesus is for the justification of the saints. *"Much more then, being now justified by His blood, we shall be saved from wrath through him."* Romans5:9. In other words, the blood cleanses us from our guilt by making us right and just before God. It presents us as people who have never committed errors in their whole lives.

The blood of Jesus is the seal of the New Testament. *"Likewise also the cup after supper, saying; 'This cup is the new testament in my blood, which is shed for you.'"* Luke 22:20. It is that which keeps our agreement with God binding and is that official stamp of approval between God and us. It is also that cohesive harmonious force existing between us and God that binds two things together that had been existing separately.

The blood of Jesus has a scriptural use of the sanctification of believers in Christ. *"And I said unto him, sir, thou knowest. And he said to me, these are they which came out of great tribulation, and have washed their robes, and made them white in the blood of the lamb."* Revelation 7:14 (KJV). We should take note here that it is not for the sanctification of properties (earthly material things), but believers (human beings who believe in the finished work of Christ). This blood has the power to cleanse, wash clean, purify and make holy a person who believes in Christ. It cleanses us from sin, iniquity, transgressions and all forms of unrighteousness.

Communion is also one of the purposes for which the blood was shed. We do use the blood of Jesus Christ in communion whereby the wine is being changed by prayers into the blood of Jesus Christ, which is then taken as a drink by believers in Christ. *"The cup of blessing which we bless, is it not the communion of the blood of Christ? The bread which we break, is it not the communion of the body of Christ?"* 1 Corinthians 10:16 (KJV). The blood is drunk after feeding on the body to rejuvenate the believer, and in compliance to the commandment of Christ which says: "Do this in remembrance of me."

The blood is also taken to gain eternal life, a union with Christ and eternal satisfaction of the soul. *"Whoso eateth my flesh and drinketh my blood, hath eternal life; and I will raise him up at the last day. For my flesh is meat indeed, and my blood is drink indeed. He that eateth my flesh and drinketh my blood, dwelleth in me, and I in him.* John 6:54-56 (KJV).

Again, it is the same blood of Jesus that gives us redemption from sin and shame. That is, the blood compensates for the bad things we have done and puts us back into favor with God. *"In whom we have redemption through his blood, the forgiveness of sins, according to the riches of his glory."* Ephesians 1:7.

The blood of Christ is also for the forgiveness of sins. Here, we should take note that forgiveness is different from remission. Remission is for one who never repented while forgiveness is for one who has repented and commits an offense. This is because remission is a deeper word in relation to cleansing than forgiveness.

Revelation 12:11 says, *"And they overcome him by blood of the Lamb, and by the word of their testimony;...* Here also, it is important to note that "the blood of the Lamb" refers the death of Jesus Christ on the cross, while "the word of their testimony" refers to their belief in that death. Thus, the scripture is saying that "they overcome the devil by the death of Christ on the cross, and by their belief in that death..." It is not talking of them using the blood of the lamb as an offensive or defensive weapon against the devil. Even if it does, this scripture alone is not enough to defend the doctrine of using the blood of Jesus as a weapon against the devil.

In fact, our spiritual security is not guaranteed solely in the blood, but in the person of Christ. Our salvation from sin, death and hell is guaranteed by the blood, but not our security in Christ. Christ himself is our security:

> *"I am the good shepherd: the good Shepherd gives his life for the Sheep. But he that is a hireling, and not the shepherd, whose own the sheep are not, sees the wolf coming, and leaves the sheep, and flees: and the wolf catches them, and scatters the sheep. The hireling flees, because he is a hireling, and cares not for the sheep. I am the good shepherd, and know my sheep, and am known of mine. And I give unto them eternal life; and they shall never perish, <u>neither shall any man pluck them out of my hand.</u>"* John 10:11-14&28 (KJV).

We have just enumerated all what the Bible tells us about the blood of Jesus. Yet, we have not been able to figure out some of those beliefs the church today has about that blood.

The body of Christ is founded on principles, Commandments, blessings and privileges. Therefore, things are not done there in a disorganized, unharmonious and haphazard manner. There is only one text book this body should use for directives and enlightenment. Consequently, anything that is not found in and taught from this book is not valid and should not be used by the body. Today, there are so many teachings about the blood of Jesus that are not in this text book, which is the Bible. We will see them one after the other.

The first thing is that the blood of Jesus today is seen by the church as an offensive weapon of warfare against the kingdom of darkness. This is scripturally wrong because when the weapons of warfare were listed in scriptures by Apostle Paul, we saw only one offensive weapon which is the word of God (the sword of the spirit) Ephesians 6:17. Secondly, there are no other places in the Bible were the blood of Jesus was used as an offensive weapon. Yet, it is a common thing today to hear men of God shouting "the blood of Jesus!" in their combat with the kingdom of darkness. I guess that is why the results are not very encouraging.

Many more in the body of Christ today do use it as a defensive weapon. "I cover myself with the blood of Jesus", "I cover my family with the blood of Jesus", "I cover my husband, the church, my children with the blood of Jesus"; are commonly heard today in the prayers of many. Unfortunately, there is nothing like the blood of Jesus under the list of defensive weapons of warfare in Ephesians 6. All we have there is the belt of truth, the breastplate of righteousness, the shoes of the gospel of peace, the shield of faith, and the helmet of salvation. Also, nowhere in scriptures are we told that the disciples used it as a defensive weapon, or gave instructions that it should be used as such. So, where has this doctrine emanated from?

First of all, anyone who is in Christ is already in the blood and body of Christ. He needs not to pray the "cover me with the blood" prayer. If anyone who is in Christ is praying thus, it means he is ignorant of his position in Christ, because you cannot be in Christ and are not covered with His blood. The "cover me with the blood" prayer is that of doubtful and unbelieving people. And as the scriptures say, those who doubt cannot receive from God (James 1:6-8), and without faith, it is impossible to please God (Hebrews 11:6).

The blood of Jesus is not anointing oil that believers should use in anointing properties. That blood has its own uses and believers should know that and be able to use it rightly. The blood was not shed for inhuman and earthly things that do not have the slightest value before God.

You can call this a crusade against the wrong use of the blood of Jesus. But all I want us to know is that, though those who use it on properties do it in the spiritual sense – without using a physical blood of Christ (which cannot even be gotten and kept physically today), it is not the blood of animals as in the days of the Passover and exodus that should be rubbed on door posts and houses and properties. In fact, even that was done by a special instruction from God. Yet, there is no such instruction from God today for the blood of Jesus to be used as such. This blood (of Jesus) is meant for the redemption, sanctification, justification, communion, and salvation of souls and nothing else.

It should also be noted that the blood of Jesus does not atone or act on somebody by petition, but by believing in the Lordship of Christ Jesus. Therefore, pleading the blood on an unrepentant family member is as good as nothing. I am not saying that you should not pray for their protection and salvation. I am highly in support of that. But what I am against is you using the blood on persons, places, things and times when it is not supposed to be used.

The blood of Jesus is no doubt powerful to save. But it should be used rightly, on those who have repented and have accepted Christ, to be sanctified, justified, purified and redeemed from all unrighteousness by that blood.

Chapter Nine

THE FEAR OF GOD

THERE ARE SO MANY SCRIPTURES, especially in the Old Testament that talk about the fear of God. And there are as well so many others especially in the New Testament that talk of the opposite to the fear of God. Here, we are going to see how the phrase "the fear of God" is applicable to our lives as children of God and in the New Testament era.

As a child of God, you ought not to be afraid of your Father God, else you will not enjoy a good father-son relationship. The Bible calls us "sons of God" not by error. A child who is afraid of the father is always scared of him, and is uncomfortable in the father's presence. But the Bible admonishes us to enter boldly into the presence of God to find Grace to help in time of need. The Bible also admonishes us to "fear not" up to 365 times.

If the people of God of Old like Abraham in the Bible were not afraid to confront God with serious issues like the destruction of

Sodom and Gomorrah, I think children of God today should be "fear free" with their heavenly Father.

Serving God in the Old Testament was characterized by a lot of fear, owing to the dreadful Holy of Holies that contained the Ark of the Covenant, and Dreadful incidences like that of Korah, Dathan and Abiram. In fact, so many fearful things happened that were able to keep the people under total fear.

Jesus came to reconcile man to God after that long separation from God at Eden. Man's disobedience and the consequent separation was one of the reasons why that fear ought to be. Sin separated man from God and brought fear into man. The very first time the word fear is found in the Bible is in Genesis 3:10, when Adam and Eve sinned against God. This means that before the unfortunate event of them disobeying God by eating the forbidden fruit, they enjoyed a fear free relationship with God.

Jesus came to re-unite man with God and take away the fear for a loving father's care to man. That is why the veil at the Temple had to be torn from top to bottom, to remove anything that could hinder man's free access to God.

Jesus did not come with the message of a dreadful God who has to be feared by all, but He came with the message of a loving Father who is willing to forgive and bless His children. When Jesus taught about "whom to fear" in Matt 10:28, His emphasis was not that we should fear God, but that we should not be afraid of the devil because he hasn't the final say of our lives; and that if at all we want to be afraid of any person, it should be God who has the final say of our lives. Yet, He did not emphasis on the message of us fearing God; that is why verse 31 of the same chapter of Matt 10 reads, "Fear ye not therefore...."

I know you may want to justify like others by saying there are many kinds of fear. And that when we talk of the fear of God, we are not talking of being scared and running away from Him, but of a holy reverence. What do you mean? There is nothing like many kinds of fear: fear is fear. And fear should not exist in any intimate relationship. The word fear does not exist in God's Kingdom. Apostle Paul tells us that we have not received the spirit of fear.

> *"For you did not received the spirit of bondage again to fear; but you received the spirit of adoption, by whom we cry, Abba father"* Romans 8:15 (NKJV).

> *"For God has not given us a spirit of fear, but of power, and of love, and of a sound mind"* 2 Timothy 1:7 (NKJV).

The Holy Spirit does not make us fear God. He rather takes us into discovering the very person of God our Father. Some people equate the Holy Spirit with the fear of God. They say "when you have the Spirit of God, it means you have the fear of God". Which is very wrong. How can you equate God (the Holy Spirit) with fear? And we should take special note that the Holy Spirit does not bring fear into us.

That is why some Old Testament scriptures have to be revised, if at all they have to be applicable in this New Testament era. And I believe by the teachings of the New Testament, those scriptures have already been revised, even though it may need some Divine illumination for us to understand that. Jesus Himself had to openly revise the Ten Commandments, the laws of Moses and some other scriptures to suit the New Testament doctrine. Revising a scripture does not mean canceling it, taking it off the Bible or declaring it not useful. Those that Jesus revised are still there and are useful.

The scripture that says "the fear of the Lord is the beginning of wisdom" (Proverbs 9:10) is one of those that are to be revised, save for its application in the New Testament. Today, it is not the fear of the Lord that brings wisdom into us, but the entrance of the Holy Spirit in our lives. We are told in scriptures that He is our teacher, and that when He shall come, He shall teach us new things. We are also told that the Holy Spirit is a Spirit of wisdom. So, to us it is the entrance of the Holy Ghost that gives us wisdom, and not the fear of the Lord.

Today, there ought to be nothing like the fear of the Lord. If at all it has to exit, it should be out of the body of Christ; because Christ is not afraid of the Father. And since we are in Christ, we cannot be afraid of God our Father.

What we are supposed to have is a holy reverence and love for God, and not fear. The Bible makes it clear that there are only two commandments of love that we have in the New Testament, which are;

> *"And you shall love the LORD your God with all thy heart, with all your soul, and with all your mind, and with all your strength. This is the first commandment. And the second, like it, is this: you shall love your*

neighbour as yourself. There is no other commandment greater than these." Mark 12:30-31 (NKJV).

If you love God with all your heart, soul, mind and strength, you will do everything to please Him, and you will not be afraid of Him. I don't think you are afraid of who you truly love. There is no other commandment that says we should be afraid of God. But if you say there is another commandment that says "fear God", you should go ahead and obey it: as for me, there is no valid commandment telling me to fear God that needs my obedience.

Fear is inhuman and dehumanizes man. When God crated man, there was nothing like fear in man. Fear came into man only after the fall at the Garden of Eden. Genesis 3:10 says *"And he said, I heard thy voice in the garden and I was afraid, because I was naked; and I hid myself".* This was the first time fear was mentioned in the Bible, and was introduced to man. Thus, fear comes not from God, but from the devil and results from sin. Fear is a product of sin, and not of righteousness.

Here was Adam, who had enjoyed a good relationship with God before the fall, and was not afraid of Him, now confessing fear. God's intension for man is not that we should fear Him, but that man should love Him. The most remote teaching you can hear in the church of the twenty first century is that which tells you to fear God.

God is love, and love and fear cannot go together. You cannot love God in fear. See what I John 4: 18 says; "There is no fear in Love; but perfect love casts out fear, because fear involves torments. But he who fears has not been made perfect in Love" (NKJV). You can read the preceding and proceeding verses for a better understanding of the above scripture. Apostle John is telling us here that those who love God are not afraid and should not be afraid of God. How can you love perfectly, if you carry fear in you?

God and fear do not live together. Fear instead causes us to run away from God, as it caused Adam to run and hid himself from God in Genesis 3:10. God cannot dwell in the life of a man who is afraid of Him. If God has to make your body His temple, you have to cast out fear from that temple.

Fear is a spirit, as seen in 2Timothy 1:7 "For God has not given us the spirit of Fear…" It is a spirit of bondage and torments. 1 John 4:18 says "fear has torments". A man (especially in an African village where the toilets are some meters away from the house) who is afraid to go out into the dark to the toilet, will be held in bondage and be tormented by fear, even to the extent of excreting on his body.

We don't approach God with fear, but with faith and boldness. Fear is part of faithlessness. He who approaches God with fear cannot please Him. Fear and faith are not compatible.

You need the opposite of fear, to be able to resist the devil and command him out of your way. You need the spirit of boldness and of a sound mind to be able to preach the gospel to the wicked. You need boldness to stand for God. You need boldness to approach the throne of Grace. You need boldness to be daring in life.

The primary root of almost every failure in life is fear, when you are afraid to invest, you cannot invest, when you are afraid of going to parliament or becoming the president, you will never be. When you are afraid of failure in any venture, you will fail. Fear is of the devil.

You need to pray and cast the fear of the Lord out of your life; and replace it with the Love of God. Pray and cast out fear in general (fear whatsoever out of your life). Take note that you have not been given a spirit of fear, but that of power, love and of a sound mind.

Wisdom does not come from the fear of the Lord, but comes from the Spirit of God., any wisdom that comes from the fear of God, is no wisdom, fake wisdom, devilish and compromising wisdom. True wisdom comes from the Spirit of God.

The fear of God's judgment is also the fear of God. In fact, it is what results to the fear of God. But many fail to understand that when you are in Christ, you need not to be afraid of God's judgment, because you have already been judged by God through Christ. That is, Christ was condemned on the cross on your behalf. Therefore, if you are now in Christ, how can Christ be judged the second time?

There is nothing for us to be afraid of in God. God's judgment has already passed over us. God's anger cannot fall on Christ, and therefore cannot fall on us.

> *"Since, therefore, [these His] children share in flesh and blood [in the physical nature of human beings], He [Himself] in a similar manner partook of the same [nature], that by [going through] death He might bring to nought and make of no effect him who had the power of death- that is, the devil- and also that He might deliver and completely set free all those who through the [hunting] fear of death were held in bondage throughout the whole course of their lives."* Hebrews 2:14-15 (Amp)

Jesus did not only come to set us free from sin, but from the slavery of fear as well. This scripture above shows us that the children of God were slaves to the fear of death all through their lives, until when Jesus showed up; and gave them their complete deliverance.

The first time I prepared this message, I could not preach it with all assurance. But when I heard pastor Chris Oyakilome saying that fear has been disabled in His life, I was encouraged. He said it was not something he thought could happen; but he just realized that there is no more fear of whatsoever in him.

You need to pray that God should disable fear in your life, and make you fear free, in Jesus' name! Amen.

Bibliography

Brand Chad, Mitchell Eric Alan, Bond Steve, Clendenen E. Ray, Butler Trent C. Latta Bill, (2015) *Holman Illustrated Bible Dictionary* (Revised and Expanded), B$H Publishing Group, Nashville Tennesse, 284.

Christine Schultz, (2021 Nov 12) *why are wedding dresses white?* Retrieved from https://www.almanac.com

Easton Matthew George, (1897) *Easton's Bible Dictionary,* Thomas Nelson Publication, 238.

Hornby A. S. (1984) *Oxford Advanced Learner's Dictionary,* (sixth edition), Oxford University Press Publication, 1075.

Janet Lomax, (2022), *The Oldest Wedding Vows.* Retrieved from https://www.weddingsido.com.au

Martha Stewart, (2021 Mar 25), *Traditional Wedding Vows for your Ceremony.* Retrieved from https://www.marthastewart.com

Smith William, (1884) *Smith's Bible Dictionary,* Grand Rapids, MI: Christian Classic Ethereal Library Publication, 180-190.

Tenny, Merril, (1963) *Zondervan Pictorial Bible Dictionary,* Grand Rapids, Zondervan Publishing House, 889.

2009 DVD, Encarta Dictionaries.Inc, Microsoft Student with Encarta Premium.